STROUD'S
GOLDEN VALLEY
IN OLD PHOTOGRAPHS

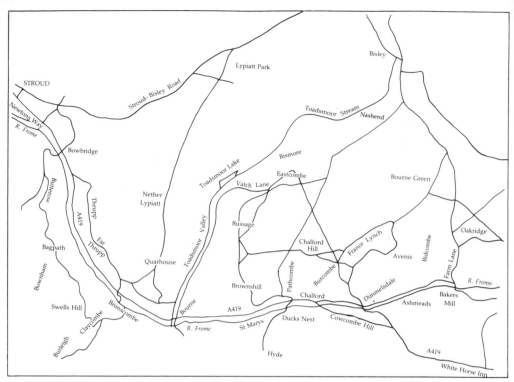

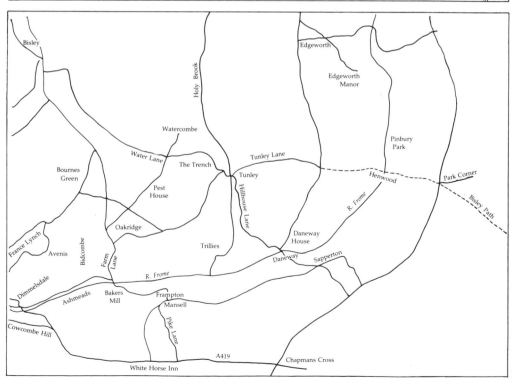

STROUD'S
GOLDEN VALLEY
IN OLD PHOTOGRAPHS

COLLECTED BY
S.J. GARDINER & L.C. PADIN

ALAN SUTTON
1989

Alan Sutton Publishing
Gloucester

First published 1989

British Library Cataloguing in Publication Data

Stroud's golden valley in old photographs.
1. Gloucestershire. Stroud. (District). [Social life, [1837–
I. Gardiner, S.J.   II. Padin, L. C.
942.4'19081

ISBN 0-86299-705-X

Typesetting and origination by
Alan Sutton Publishing
Printed in Great Britain by
Dotesios Printers Limited

CONTENTS

DANEWAY 1911. The west portal of the canal tunnel. A party of trippers emerging from a trip inside the tunnel. Note the lantern on the bow. Seated with arms folded is Mr Stephens from Brimscombe. Two of the young ladies are the Misses Clemance from Chalford.

INTRODUCTION

Stroud's Golden Valley is only one of several Golden Valleys. The best known in Gloucestershire now is probably that between Gloucester and Cheltenham, solely because it has given its name to the dual-carriageway link between the two. Before Local Government re-organization in 1974 there was another one in the Bitton Area of South Gloucestershire. Then, of course, there is the well-known Golden Valley in Herefordshire. However, rightly or wrongly, in our view Stroud's Golden Valley is *the* Golden Valley.

It is the valley of the River Frome, or Stroudewater as it is named in many old deeds and estate maps, to the east of Stroud. Even then this is not strictly correct for the true Golden Valley starts at the east end of Chalford and continues east and north to its upper levels above Edgeworth. This is the relatively unspoilt, undeveloped part of the valley, somewhat alpine in character, still well-wooded with deciduous trees which give it an autumn beauty unsurpassed in the Cotswolds.

The name 'Golden Valley' is not a fairly modern description in spite of the story that, on a train journey through the valley, Queen Victoria, remarking on the autumn tints of the woods, called it a golden valley. Neither does it result from the answer of F.W. Street, top-link driver of the GWR before the last war, when asked which was his favourite run out of Paddington. His reply was that the run from Swindon to Cardiff via Gloucester was his favourite and the best part was on leaving Sapperton Tunnel to run down the valley to Stroud in autumn. In fact, the name had been applied to it more than two centuries earlier and, in 1784, a Reeves rating account listed several living in the Brownshill – Chalford area under the heading 'the part from the Bourn to the Goulden Valley'. Let Mary Rudd, in *Historical Records of Bisley* (1), have the last say:

'Year by year Nature justifies this name when the trees of the vale are clothed with their favourite autumn tints, but whether arising from this poetic source, or from the fortunes made by the numerous clothiers of the valleys, remains a moot point.'

For the purposes of this book the area covered commences to the east of central Stroud at the junction of the new by-pass – Newton's Way – with London Road, continuing south-east, east and north to embrace the civil parishes of Thrupp, Chalford, Bisley and Sapperton, together with the northern fringes of Rodborough and Minchinhampton parishes. Because the fortunes of this area were closely linked with the ancient parish of Bisley, which included Stroud itself, no record such as this can be entire unless the Toadsmoor Valley and the combes and villages on the edges of the Frome Valley are included. Sapperton parish is equally as ancient and, in the upper reaches of the valley, each influenced the other. It gave its name to the Craft School, set up at the beginning of this century by Ernest Gimson and the Barnsley Brothers to follow the ideas of William Morris which were, basically, to keep alive the handcraft skills rapidly disappearing under the Victorian Industrial Revolution. Somewhat similar to the upsurge in the arts and crafts which we experience today.

Life in the area at that time was, lightheartedly, described by Norman Jewson, who came into the area to work with Ernest Barnsley, in his book *By chance I did Rove*. (6) Although, through TV and radio programmes, the Valley is becoming widely known for its beauty and relative tranquillity, one can only hope that it will remain unspoilt and not be subjected to a surfeit of tourism and all its gimicky impedimenta.

Once again we have sifted through our collection to try to present an interesting and balanced view of the Valley and its environs. Even then, the selection printed herein has only been achieved after much heart-searching over what to put in and what to leave out. Views showing the Great Western Railway and the Thames and Severn Canal have only been included where they will show aspects of the Valley and the life of the area, or serve as reference points. Both have been well-documented in two other books in this series (2 & 3) which supplement this book to some extent. Similarly, only where necessary to achieve continuity in this pictorial journey have views of the villages of the Golden Valley, previously included in the two books of Old Photographs of the Stroud area (4 & 5), been used. Wherever appropriate we have included historical information in the captions.

Finally, to those readers who are not well acquainted with this lovely Golden Valley come and explore it. By foot is best, but treat it with the respect it deserves and don't hanker after its commercialization.

(1) *Historical Records of Bisley*. Mary Rudd. Alan Sutton Publishing.
(2) *Stroud Road and Rail in Old Photographs*. Alan Sutton Publishing.
(3) *The Stroudwater and Thames & Severn Canals in Old Photographs*. Alan Sutton Publishing.
(4) *Stroud and the Five Valleys in Old Photographs*. Alan Sutton Publishing.
(5) *Stroud and the Five Valleys in Old Photographs: A Second Selection*. Alan Sutton Publishing.
(6) *By chance I did Rove*. Norman Jewson. Published privately.

From Stroud to the Bourne

This section covers the widest part of the Golden Valley and, at this present time, the most industrialized section. Here there was sufficient room on the valley floor to keep the railway, canal and road reasonably far apart, with the three only joining forces as The Bourne is reached. Now it has become residential enough to warrant inclusion in the Stroud overall development plan. Yet it is still so rural in many respects that it cannot be classed as true suburbia.

THE JUNCTION OF FIELD ROAD AND LONDON ROAD, Stroud c. 1908. Upper Dorington Terrace is on the left and Lower Dorington Terrace is on the right. Both are late nineteenth-century developments of artisans' houses. These followed on the creation of Field Road, some 30 years earlier, to link upper Stroud with London Road, utilising a short section of the old rough cart track down Spring Road. The road opposite the cart gave access to the Midland Railway Yard and station at Wallbridge. The present London Road – Newton's Way roundabout – is where the wall curves on the left.

THE VIEW NORTH-WEST from the Butterow railway bridge over Arundel's Mill which would have been the Dye-houses of Gyde-Bishop & Co. in c. 1905–10. The two Dorrington Terraces are prominent on the right. On the same level, the low black building over the curve of the canal is the Midland Railway Stables where carts, fodder, etc., were stored on the ground floor and the horses went up a ramp to the stables on the upper floor. The white oblongs are the stable doorways.

THE VIEW ACROSS ARUNDEL'S MILL POND to London and Park Roads, c. 1900–10. Dirleton House, now behind Coulter's Garage, is on the left and was, for many years, the home of Dr Waller. Most of the development between the two roads has taken place in the last 40 years.

BOWBRIDGE from the railway halt c. 1900–5. A vastly different view to that seen from the same spot today. The area to the right of the road has been re-developed with the arrival of the Veterinary Surgery, the Bowbridge Lock Estate, Lacey & Thompson's Garage, Webbs lorry park and Pooles Garage. In October 1940 a Hurricane fighter crashed between the London Road and the four-storey mill building on the right. The building itself was burnt down some years later. The terrace and cottages on the opposite side of the road were demolished for road widening some 25 years ago.

BUTTEROW FROM THE HORNS with Mount Vernon partly hidden in the trees (upper right) c. 1910–15. The Pike House can be seen over the second house on the right.

THE VIEW FROM BUTTEROW across the valley to Near Thrupp c. 1910. The mill is Stafford's Mill, now a small industrial estate. A mill has been on this site since the sixteenth century when Richard Stafforde was making cloth there. The Stanton family owned the mill from 1793 to the 1880s as a working woollen mill. It was later taken over by S.G. Bailey for the manufacture of paints, their speciality being manganese-based products. Some 25 years ago it closed, the name being retained by a paint-factoring business, set up in the adjoining Griffins Mill, by some of the management.

A SMALL COLLECTION OF HOUSES on the south side of the valley clustered near Bagpath House from where this photograph was taken c. 1910–20. The road in the foreground was the old road from Stroud to Brimscombe via Butterow. Here it is approaching Querkins Corner from where a footpath descends to Phoenix canal bridge (p. 14).

THE VIEW EAST FROM BUTTEROW TO BRIMSCOMBE (upper right), c. 1930, with the Thames & Severn Canal still in working order, while a distant puff of steam suggests that the railcar is *en route* between Ham Mill and Brimscombe Bridge Halts. Note the pronounced eastward curve of the valley. The building on the extreme left is the old Malakoff Inn, the mill to its right being Griffins Mill. The next mill is Ham Mill and, beyond the trees, is the Phoenix Ironworks.

THE OPPOSING VIEW down the valley to Stroud from Wallsquarry c. 1905–10. Centre right, the house at the end of the terrace was the Phoenix Inn, now an antique furniture salesroom. Bottom right, between the trees, is Phoenix Bridge, recently restored by the county council.

THE VIEW NORTH-WEST along the Canal from Hope Mill (or Ridlers) Lock to Phoenix Bridge, 1943. In the distance, slightly left of the bridge, is Ham Mill Halt.

14

FAR THRUPP viewed from the railway c. 1905–13. The buildings lower right are part of the Phoenix Ironworks of George Waller & Sons. These works were probably built on the site of an earlier woollen mill. It was at this works, when they were owned by John Ferrabee, that Edwin Budding designed and built the first lawn-mower (now in Stroud Museum). Power Plants now occupy the field area bottom right.

ADJACENT TO HOPE MILL LOCK extensive river-boat building was carried on for almost 60 years until the Second World War; first by Edwin Clark and then by Abdela & Mitchell. The boats were launched into the canal and were usually trialled on the canal above Hope Mill Lock where this photograph was taken. The 15 de Novembro was a 60 ft steel vessel, steam-powered and a quarter-wheeler. The name suggests it was built for use in Brazil. Photograph c. 1912.

THIS VIEW DOWN THE VALLEY from Brimscombe Church shows how the valley curves in a long arc from Stroud to Brimscombe c. 1873/4. Centre left is Hope Mills then, possibly, both a silk and a woollen mill. In the centre is Brimscombe Lower Mills, with the Upper Mills to the right, both of which were worked by the Evans family. The three-gabled house to the right is the Mill House, or Biggs Place.

BRIMSCOMBE CANAL BRIDGE viewed from Brimscombe Corner in 1911. It was a typical canal hump-backed bridge and had a large gas main strapped to the arch on both sides. Behind the trees on the left there was once a small gasometer. The Ship Inn is to the right.

THE VIEW FROM THE BRIDGE towards Brimscombe Port c. 1930. Brimscombe Polytechnic is over the shed to the right. The right-hand towpath led to the West Wharf, the left-hand one to the main road opposite the Port Inn. To the right of this path, as it curves, can be seen the rear of Brimscombe Co-op Stores.

THE VIEW FROM WHARF ROAD c. 1910. The small shop on the left was once Brimscombe Post Office. The cottage on the right was the home of Mr Ernest Barrett, the last Chief of Brimscombe Fire Brigade. The gabled house over the bridge is Biggs Place.

THE BOTTOM OF BRIMSCOMBE HILL from the Canal bridge, the entrance to Port Mills being on the left, c. 1920s. The finger post pointed to the road to the West Wharf and Lugg's Foundry.

THE VIEW FROM THE CANAL MAINTENANCE YARD across Brimscombe Basin to the West Wharf and Victoria Road c. 1905–10. The Port Mill on the right remains today. The left-hand building in front was the lengthman's cottage and has now been demolished; the right-hand building was the Salt Store and remains today as the sole survivor of the Canal Wharf buildings. Centre left is the gable end of the Wesleyan Chapel, with the church on the skyline above.

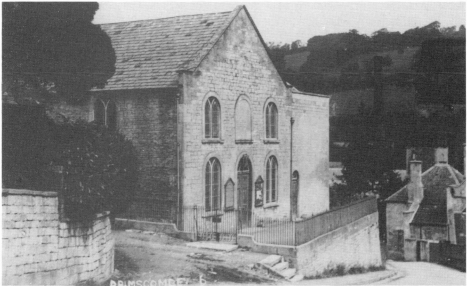

BRIMSCOMBE WESLEYAN CHAPEL, c. 1910–20, built around 1820. The building stands just to the south-east of the shortest tunnel on the old GWR, the bridge immediately preceding it being on the lower right of the picture. It is said that, when the railway was constructed in 1841–5, the tunnel was bored out rather than making a deep cutting so that the Chapel foundations would not be undercut.

BRIMSCOMBE CHURCH OF THE HOLY TRINITY c. 1910–20. A meeting was called at the Ship Inn on 2 January 1837 to consider the best means of erecting a church at Brimscombe. Mr John George of Brimscombe gave the land, Mr David Ricardo of Gatcombe Park endowed the edifice and the Revd William Cocking laid the foundation stone on 20 June 1839. The year of erection is incorporated in the weather vane on the top of the tower.

THE VIEW FROM THE ORCHARDS towards Brimscombe Pike c. 1910. The upper road – Orchard Lane – leads from Goughs Orchard Canal Bridge to Brimscombe Hill just below the Pike. The lower lane leads across the Moors to Swells Hill and is at the bottom of Claycombe, the little combe running up to Burleigh. Housing developments of the past 40 years now cover the fields.

A VIEW OF SWELLS HILL IN WINTER from the north-west side of the valley c. 1910. The old road from Butterow to Brimscombe passes behind the house on the right and continues left along Watery Lane to Brimscombe Pike. Bownham Park House is seen faintly in the trees on the skyline.

THE VIEW ACROSS THE CATTLE POND at Blackditch to Wallsquarry and Brimscombe, showing how the valley curves at St Marys, c. 1905. Centre left, the tall building is Brimscombe Polytechnic. This cattle pond is still visible in a very delapidated state alongside the road from Bownham to Burleigh.

THE VIEW ACROSS UPPER CLAYCOMBE from below The Knoll to Burleigh c. 1910. The square building, upper centre, was the Lodge House at the driveway entrance to Burleigh Court.

THE VIEW FROM THE CEMETERY towards Brimscombe Corner (left) c. 1873/4. Centre right is the headquarters building of the Thames & Severn Canal with the Basin and West Wharf in front. Lower centre is Port Mills and the mill building to its left was the old Silk Mill. This had a separate chimney some distance behind and above presumably to give a better draft. The mill, which had belonged to the Evan's family, is now Gordon Terrace, housing the village shops. The house to the left was the Mill Managers' House and is now the post office.

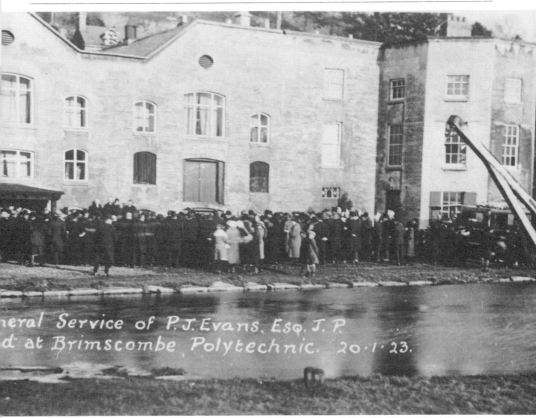

ieral Service of P.J. Evans, Esq. J.P.
d at Brimscombe Polytechnic. 20·1·23.

A MEMBER OF THE EVANS FAMILY of Brimscombe Mills – Edward Holt Evans – started evening classes so that the young men of Brimscombe could further their education around 1889. This was the start of Brimscombe Polytechnic in which the Evans family always took a keen interest, as can be seen in this photograph when the funeral service of P.J. Evans, a long serving Governor, was held here in 1923. The work of the Polytechnic centred on the old T & S Headquarters building, although part was accommodated in the Lower Mills (see the next photograph). The building was eventually renovated to give better facilities and was ceremonially reopened in 1911 by the Duchess of Beaufort (pp. 136).

BRIMSCOMBE POLYTECHNIC but not the well-known canal basin building c. 1906/7. This photograph shows that the Polytechnic also occupied the part of Brimscombe Lower Mills nearest the main road. It is surmised that the photograph shows where the 'Thrupp/ Brimscombe Craft School opened on Sept. 3rd 1906 in buildings used by Brimscombe Polytechnic for 50 boys, of the age of 12, selected from neighbouring Elementary Schools'. It was eventually to form the basis of the Craft School, later the Boys Central, then Boys Technical, and now the Junior School of Marling School, at Downfield.

THE VIEW FROM THE WEST WHARF across the island to Bourne (Hacks) Mill c. 1910–20. The Basin formed the trans-shipment port for goods to be transferred between the wide boats of the Severn and the narrow boats of the Thames, the island forming a relatively theft proof storage area.

THE VIEW FROM BRIMSCOMBE CEMETERY across the Basin and T & S Canal Maintenance Yard 1873/4. Houses now cover most of the lower fields. Quarhouse is in the upper right of the picture.

SWING THE CAMERA SLIGHTLY TO THE EAST and the view is over Bourne Mills and Bourne House with Brimscombe Station and Goods Yard centre right in 1873/4. The line on the left marks the limit of the previous photograph.

Brimscombe Valley.

A SIMILAR VIEW around 60 years later in the 1930s. Comparison of the two pictures shows how the Bourne area had developed. Brownshill is on the skyline with the footpath, linking it to Brimscombe Station, crossing Brownshill Banks.

THE BOURNE and the entrance to the Toadsmore Valley viewed from The Knapp c. 1920. Lower left is the mill pond of Dark Mills. Across the road is the gasometer of Brimscombe Gas Works, the pit of which is now a cooling water reservoir for Critchley's Wimberley Mill Works.

ANOTHER VIEW FROM THE KNAPP, this time slightly to the east over Brimscombe Station Goods Shed c. 1910–20. The present-day widened and realigned A419 passes over the site of the shed. The mill chimney on the left is that of Lewiston Mill, at the entrance to the Toadsmoor Valley, with Quarhouse on the skyline above.

THE VIEW FROM BROWNSHILL BANKS over Brimscombe Station to Wimberley Mills and The Knapp, with a goods train pulling into the station to take on the banker c. 1930. The square building, bottom left, is the Victoria (now The King & Castle) Hotel.

THE VIEW EAST FROM BRIMSCOMBE STATION FOOTBRIDGE to St Marys c. 1955. The building on the left is the Banker Shed. The stretch of the T & S Canal above Beales Lock was always kept in good order as it provided water for the Banker Shed tank. Brimscombe station was opened in 1845 and served as a station for the surrounding villages.

The Toadsmoor Valley to Bisley

To introduce the reader to this valley a few verses from a poem found in a penny baker's bread book, entitled 'A poetical description of the Romantic Vale of Toadsmore, by Thomas Millard, 1831' have been included.

Arise, my powers; awake, my muse,
Let truth itself direct my views,
While on this spot I pore.
Help with precision to describe,
Above all fear, without a bribe,
The narrow vale of 'Toadsmore.'

Should any stranger ever venture,
On this romantic vale to enter,
To view the landscape o'er;
Let such with caution mark the way,
And turn quite north when at the quay,
For that's the way to 'Toadsmore.'

Quite near the place, be soon or late,
You'll sure to find a turnpike gate,
No need of saying more.
The first place here is called the Bourn,
Where many dance, while others mourn,
But we'll pass on to 'Toadsmore.'

(And, finally, as Bisley comes in sight)

Next we behold our Bisley steeple,
Built to attract all sorts of people,
The wealthy and the poor;
There meet the learned and the rude,
Each hopes to find some solid good,
That is not found in 'Toadsmore'.

THE ENTRANCE TO THE TOADSMOOR VALLEY at the rear of Lewiston Mill c. 1910–20. The workers in the foreground might be doing some repair work to the mill pond. The stone wall is alongside the Toadsmoor road to Eastcombe. The houses on the hill are the Blackness part of Upper Bourne and the old road from Stroud to Chalford passed along the sunken lane to the left of the field.

THE NEXT SECTION OF THE ROAD past Gussage Mill (left) c.1910–20. The mill had connections with the wood-turning trade for more than a century but it closed some years ago and it is now owned by Savages the Builders. It was from this mill that William Dangerfield moved his walking stick business to Bliss Mills at Chalford, around 1860, to become Chalford's biggest employer (employing over 1000 hands). The move was something of a festive occasion with all the employees, led by a band, marching with flags and banners from Gussage to Bliss Mills. STB Engineering now occupy the patchwork quilt site below the mill.

THE TOADSMOOR ROAD NEAR SELWYNS MILL, C. 1910, where present-day road widening is taking place. The people are obviously posed for the photographer, with the governess cart stopped and a passenger (?) sitting on the verge. The road is no longer as peaceful as this today, having become a commuter race track.

SELWYNS MILL, Bussage, situated near the junction of Bussage Hill and Toadsmoor Road, c. 1880–1900. The mill had been known as Snow's, Hayward's and Toadsmoor Mill. This photograph shows the Upper Mill which was powered by a leat running from a small pond north of the track to Nether Lypiatt Manor. A small pond has recently been reconstructed there. The building on the right was the Mill House which is still standing. The small building in the left foreground is now Hampton Colours, but the rest were demolished many years ago. The mill had been used as a woollen and a flock mill.

PART OF TOADSMOOR, the lane on the right leading up to Toadsmoor Garage at the foot of the Vatch c. 1910. The house, bottom right, is all that remains of the Wiselands Mill buildings. This was a sixteenth-century mill, derelict by 1800 and demolished soon afterwards. The large flat area on the left is the remains of the mill pond, the Toadsmoor stream running behind the embankment.

THE VIEW NORTH ACROSS TOADSMOOR LAKE to the Woodmans (now Keepers) Cottage c. 1910. The cottage was built on a high bank, by Sir John Dorington of Lypiatt Manor, to avoid occasional flooding which sometimes happened to the Keepers Cottage at Bismore (p. 39). The lake was the old Fishpond for Lypiatt Manor.

BUSSAGE CHURCH from the north-west c. 1900; the second church to be built by Thomas Keble the Elder, Vicar of Bisley, in 1844–6. Because of the probable instability of the site, it had to be supported on the north wall by oak piles. The church owed its foundation to 20 Oxford scholars who, in 1839, pledged to set aside £20 per year for 5 years to build a church which should be 'substantial, beautiful and handsomely adorned'.

THE VIEW FROM BUSSAGE CHURCH over Bussage Hill to the Glebe House (Vicarage), top left, c. 1910. The lane in the centre leads from Bussage Hill to the Ram Inn on The Ridge. Applegarth is on the right.

A VIEW DOWN THE LANE in the previous photograph to the church c. 1910. There appears to be a goat occupying the road.

BUSSAGE GLEBE HOUSE as The Vicarage c. 1906–10. It is believed that the figures in the doorway are the Revd H.F. Hayward, his wife and daughter, hence the date.

THE RAM INN, Bussage c. 1900–5. If the date is correct then the figure in the gateway could be the landlord – Harry Wall – and the boy, his son Jack (p. 137).

EASTCOMBE VILLAGE GREEN, C. 1910, in not quite such a well-kept state as it is today. The lady on the right is standing at the gate of the post office of those days and is probably Mrs Antill.

A VIEW IN EASTCOMBE from Dr Crouch's Road near The Triangle down the road to Bismore, c. 1910. Berwick House garden wall is on the right.

THE VIEW APPROXIMATELY NORTH-WEST over The Street area of Eastcombe across the Toadsmoor Valley towards Ferris Court, c. 1905–10. The end-on building, bottom centre, is Model Cottages, with Rose Cottage to its right. Note the seemingly haphazard way the cottages are perched on the hillside, blending in with a perfectly natural look, but a modern planner's nightmare.

THE OPPOSITE VIEW to the previous one with The Street climbing towards the Lamb Inn on the skyline, c. 1906–10.

KEEPERS COTTAGE, Bismore, at the time of the sale of the Lypiatt Estate in 1919.

BISMORE, in the Toadsmoor valley below Eastcombe, 1880 or earlier.

A PHOTOGRAPH from c. 1910.

COMPARE THESE TWO PHOTOGRAPHS taken from approximately the same spot. The cottage to the left of the tree has been demolished, while that in the centre (now Fairview) has been completely restyled. The cottage, above right, – Honeyhill – shows little change. Upper centre, in the distance, is Keepers Cottage. (See the previous photograph.)

CRICKETY MILL, Lower Nashend, Bisley, c. 1905–15. It is believed to be one of the five mills in Bisley Hundred mentioned in the Domesday Book. It is the first mill down the Toadsmoor stream and stood adjacent to the old road from Bisley to Nashend and the Old Common. It probably started life as a grist mill, later a fulling mill, reverting to a grist mill and then becoming a small brewery. The last brewer and malster was one Miller Hazell who had 15 children. Before the end of the nineteenth century brewing had ceased and the building reverted to use as a private house.

THE CHANTRY, Bisley, as it was at the sale of the Lypiatt Estate in 1919. The oldest part of the building is that to the right of the porch and may be part of the 'mansion' of the original chantry priests. Their job appeared to be to assist the vicar and educate the young. After the Dissolution of the Monasteries the building passed through a succession of owners and became part of the Lypiatt Estate by 1847. Immediately prior to that it had been a farmhouse of about 60 acres. Sir John Dorington restored the house, adding gabled front rooms to the south front.

THE OLD WHITE HART INN in Wells Road, Bisley, c. 1910, now Hartwell.

THE VIEW ALONG WELLS ROAD from the gate of the Old Bakery (now Pax House) to the rear of the White Hart c. 1910–20.

VIEW FROM HOLLOWAY ROAD, Bisley, across the valley to the Old Bakery (right) and, behind, Wells Cottage in the early 1920s.

THE OPPOSITE VIEW to the previous photograph taken from the field adjoining Wells Cottage in 1911. Lower right is Back Lane and, where the dark trees are, the small Roman Catholic Church of St Mary of the Angels which was built in 1931. On the centre skyline the roof of the Rectory Tithe Barn can be seen (p. 54).

BISLEY. The steps which lead from Wells Road to the churchyard c. 1910. The restoration carried out in 1896 appeared to involve a relaying of worn steps, with some new ones added after they had been in a dangerous condition for at least 40 years. In later life, Mrs Raymond-Barker, wife of a visiting clergyman, recalled that, in 1854, they were in such a state that, as there were about 39 of them, they were compared with the 39 Articles because some of them were so difficult to negotiate.

THE BISLEY WELLS C. 1905. Once the public water supply for Bisley, it is the source of the Toadsmoor stream. The Wells were restored when the church was reconstructed, the new conduit being to the design of William Lowder. The original five spouts were increased to seven. The former were supplied from a spring under the churchyard, the new ones from a spring in Inakers field. In addition there were three troughs for washing purposes, a horse pond and a cattle trough. The new conduit was opened on 19 May 1863, with an Ascension Day Parade, and the ceremony has been perpetuated every year since. A collateral object was the commemoration of the marriage of the Prince and Princess of Wales (later Edward VII and Queen Alexandra). This is commemorated in the monogram AEA and the Prince of Wales feathers in the canopies. The masonry carries the inscription 'O ye wells bless ye the Lord, praise Him and magnify Him forever'.

THE WELLS, C. 1910–20. The washing troughs, etc., are on the left. The house on the right was the home of Major, the Bisley photographer. The blacksmith's forge is among the trees on the left.

WELLS ROAD, Bisley, 1915. An opposing view to the previous photograph. On the right is the Old Forge; Mr Davis was the last blacksmith to use it. Wells Cottage is on the right in the background.

THE BELL INN at the junction of Wells Road and High Street, Bisley, in the early 1900s. The decorations could be for the 1902 or 1911 coronations but the latter is preferred as the sign of the Bell appears to be missing. It is thought that the man with two sticks is Mr Shergold who was the landlord. The building is now the Meeting Room of the Bisley branch of the British Legion and also a branch surgery of the Eastcombe Doctors' practice.

THE JUNCTION OF HOLLOWAY ROAD AND WELLS ROAD, Bisley, c. 1920s. The front building has now been demolished. Note the petrol pump globe beyond the cottage. Petrol was supplied by Alf Chesterman.

HOLLOWAY ROAD in winter c. 1905, viewed from Rectory Farmhouse. Two of the snowballing boys are wearing Bisley Blue Coat School uniform. At the far end of the road is the Bell Inn with, above on the skyline, the Vicarage. Note the streetlight over the door of the cottage. Alf Chesterman's petrol pumps were in the garden on the left.

STREET, BISLEY, GLOS.

THE HIGH STREET from the Bell Inn c. 1900–10. Note the cobbled gutters. The building on the right carrying the streetlight was once the Brittania Inn. In 1870 'Miller' Hazell (p. 40) applied for a Spirits licence but was only given the option of transferring the licence from the Brewers Arms at Brattons, which he chose to retain. Both inns closed soon afterwards. The next building is the Court House built by Sir John Dorington to replace the old one which is now the Bear Inn. It stands on the site of the Old Market House, built in around 1735. Dorington used the round support columns of the latter in the building of Eastcombe Manor Farm Barn. Eventually the Court House passed into the hands of the Trustees of the John Taylor Educational Trust who sold it in the 1960s as its upkeep proved a bottomless drain on the charity's resources.

THE VIEW FROM THE LYCH-GATE down Church Hill to the High Street, 1913. Mr Fawkes by the gate.

WINTER 1962/3. Having heard of the Relief of Mafeking, here is a view of the Relief of Bisley after being cut off for several days by the heavy snowfalls.

LOOKING DOWN GEORGE STREET to the George Inn from the old Lock-up 1915. Sometimes the road is called Bear Pitch, from the Bear Inn at the top. The George Inn, then a Nailsworth Brewery House, is now the post office and village stores. Note another street-lamp on the house on the left, where the sign shows lamp oil is sold.

STROUD ROAD to the Bear Inn (on the right) c. 1900–5. Mr & Mrs Brunsdon are carrying the pails while Mrs Thomas Rowe looks on in the background. Mr Rowe was a wheelwright and had premises at the rear of the inn.

A PRINT OF OLD BISLEY CHURCH, c. 1836/7, showing some of the numerous outside staircases, erected by wealthy pew owners to gain access to their pews through 'windows' as Thomas Keble the Elder called them. On the left is the thirteenth-century well head which contained the poor souls light. There are several tales concerned with the medieval interdict which forbade burials at Bisley for around two years. The most probable is that a chantry priest, summoned to a dying parishioner on a dark night, tripped and fell into the well. This act resulted in the excommunication of Bisley so that Bisley dead had to be carried to Bibury for burial in the churchyard there, in the 'Bisley Piece'.

THE PRIESTS' DOOR in the thirteenth-century canopy in the south chancel wall c.1860. This was blocked up in the 1860 restoration and the effigy of a knight, formerly on an altar tomb in the south aisle, was placed in it. The effigy was replaced inside the church in the subsequent restoration of 1960. The knight may have been of the de Bisley family.

THE CHURCH, Bisley, after rebuilding c. 1920. The restoration/reconstruction of the old church began with the chancel in 1851 but the major work took place in 1860–2 the church being re-opened in July 1862. Note that the new roof has been raised and the roof form of the south aisle altered.

THE PRESENT STIRRUP CUP INN c. 1905–10. The brewery sign above the horse carriage shows that the New Inn was a house of Godsells Brewery of Salmon Springs, Stroud. The landlord's sign over the door shows that the new landlord, Harry Skinner, has recently taken over from his father. The two boys are wearing Bisley Blue Coat School uniform; the four children probably being Harry's offspring.

THE OLD TITHE BARN, Bisley, in Hayedge Lane 1913. It is separated from the farmhouse, which stands some 150 yds to the south, abutting Holloway Road. The road around it was the old road from Stroud to Cirencester via Bisley, Waterlane, Tunley, Henwood, Park Corner and across Cirencester Park along the Bisley Path to Cecily Hill at Cirencester.

The Bourne to Ashmeads

East from The Bourne the valley begins to narrow rapidly as it approaches St Marys and Chalford and the road, rail and canal only occupy the valley floor together as far as St Marys. There, the railway begins the long climb up Sapperton Bank and, half a mile further on, the road also leaves the valley climbing its south-east slope up Cowcombe Hill. Thus, for the next mile to Bakers Mill, only the canal and village road share the valley floor. It may be as well to reflect here what might have happened if commercial panic had not prompted the GWR to finally buy out The Thames & Severn Canal in the 1880s to prevent the Midland Railway from building a competitive line along the course of the canal. Chalford is now the easternmost bastion of industry in the valley.

We start this section with Brownshill because this village stood on the old cart road from Stroud via the Bourne to Chalford.

BROWNSHILL c. 1905. The Little House corner with Jubilee Terrace beyond. Note the dirt road. Many of the hill village roads were not tarmaced until the late 1920s.

BROWNSHILL c. 1910. The post office at the east end of Jubilee Terrace. It was a village general stores as well as a post office. Across the road The Pitch connects the Terrace with the lower St Marys Way (see the next photograph).

BROWNSHILL – ST MARYS WAY in the early 1930s. Brother John is standing outside Templewood. The house stood on the site of two ruined cottages which was purchased by three ladies in c. 1892. They also bought two fields from the adjacent Firwood Estate to form a small estate called Tanglewood, later Templewood. This house was built in the gardens of the two old cottages. During the excavations for this, traces of a medieval chapel were found. Tragedy struck in March 1946 when a Lancaster bomber, with full tanks, crashed on the house which was completely gutted. The crew were killed and Brother John was severely burnt.

TWO VIEWS ALONG ST MARYS WAY (c. 1910–20 and late 1930s) towards Skaiteshill from the Catholic Church of St Mary of the Angels. Apart from tree growth, little has altered except for the building, extreme left, of the Rest Home of St Raphaels. It was built in 1937 by the Misses Hudson & Kessler who, in 1935, had had the Catholic church built.

SKAITESHILL c. 1905. The old cart road from Stroud to Chalford, after leaving Brownshill and within a few hundred yards of Chalford Church. The side of Skaiteshill House can be seen through the trees on the left.

ST MARYS c. 1932/4. The A419 from St Marys corner towards the old Silk Mill (over bus). There is no need for the cyclist or the children to worry about traffic. The first house on the left is the Carpenters Arms. The square building to the right of the bus was Clayfields Mill, the roadside part of which was used by the Bennett Bros. for their wheelwrights business (p. 143). The canal bridge is Iles Bridge and there is a reasonable amount of water in the canal which was still in use as far as the Round House (by the tall mill chimney).

THE VIEW EAST from Skaiteshill (p. 58) along the valley to the foot of Cowcombe Hill c. 1920. Centre, the square house is Belvedere House with Chalford (Ballingers, Belvedere, Clarks) Mill behind. The house and the field in front is now part of the Belvedere Mews Estate. To the left of the mill chimney is the Canal Round House and, beyond, is Bliss Mills – now Chalford Industrial Estate. The cluster of houses on the right were known as the Ducks Nest and abutted the road at the bottom of Hyde Hill. They were demolished around 50 years ago.

CHALFORD c. 1905. The view north from the Ducks Nest, over Chalford Mill and the church, to Skiveralls on Chalford Hill. Note the square chimney of the mill which was replaced with a round one in the 1920s; also the row of buildings to the left of the church which was demolished for road widening around 1962. A small stream crosses the large field, upper right, and once powered five mills before joining the River Frome. The uppermost mill was the Little Mill (p. 64).

CHALFORD CHURCH viewed from the Roundhouse Wharf c. 1910. The building by the tree was part of Taysum's Blacksmithy (p. 143). The tall support wall of the road, built in 1815 when the road was made, is still there buried under the present widened road. Soil was just tipped over it into the canal to form the present embankment.

THE VIEW SOUTH from above Dark Lane over Bliss Mills – New Mill is in the centre, c. 1905. The saw-tooth-roofed building and clock tower replaced an older building destroyed by fire in 1888. The large house beyond this building and New Mill was the Old Coffee Tavern.

A CLOSE-UP of the Old Coffee Tavern c. 1900–10. It was a house with a chequered history. According to the dialect stories of Jarge Jenkins: 'Vust uv all that wuz a dye-ouz, then a pub, then a Koffy tavern, then Radical cumitty roo-ums, then a bloomin wreck, and now 'tiz a memry'. It was demolished around 1922, much of the stone being used to build Edgemont in Pooles Ground.

A WINTER VIEW north-west from the railway, c. 1925, over Bliss Mills to the Old Neighbour-hood and the entrance to Pathcombe; a little combe running up to the old Bisley Common at present-day Middle Hill Farm. Upper right is Corpus Christi Cottage; centre right — The Hollies — another of the five mills on the little stream. To its left is Millswood where, last century, there was a Swedenborgian Chapel. In the centre is Christ Church School.

ACROSS THE OLD NEIGHBOURHOOD ROAD from Corpus Christi Cottage, c. 1920s, is the old gabled tudor house now altered in outline, by renovation over some 40 years, into cottages. It was Chalford's Vicarage until the present one was built last century. The road was cut in around the 1820s to link Bisley with the new turnpike road from Stroud, by Chalford Church. When digging out this road, at about this spot, the navvies found a wall with a bricked-up recess in which there was the skeleton of a young girl.

CHALFORD HILL c. 1910–15. Abnash is the western extremity of the old Bisley Tithing of Aveniss, or Abbenesse. Abnash House, in the trees, is on an upper level of Pathcombe and is a very old house, much added to and altered. It has had connections with clothiers and farming for centuries. The road is that from Brownshill to Chalford Hill.

A TELESCOPIC VIEW of Chalford Hill from Hyde area over upper Dark Lane (left) in the late 1930s. The photograph clearly shows how these lynch villages of the Golden Valley developed piecemeal on the edge of the Lord's Common. To the lower right is the area known as Marle Hill, actually the lower part of another small combe – Burcombe. The right-hand house of the two was once a small mill and, between the two runs, the stepped path known as Jacob's Ladder.

NO PHOTOGRAPH HAS BEEN DISCOVERED of this part of upper Dark Lane just below Skiveralls that can be classed as 'old'. This recent one (1975) is included because the structure on the left is the remains of the loading platform for the Little Mill.

BURCOMBE, Chalford Hill c. 1910–15. The Eastcombe & Bisley road from Brantwood Crossroads. The wall on the left surrounded a piece of garden ground until about 40 years ago when it was purchased by the County Council and the wall demolished to give better visibility. It is now Brantwood Green. The remaining view has altered considerably with housing development on both sides of the road.

CHALFORD HILL c. 1933–6. The road leading from Queens Square to Randalls Green – Carters Road. At that time the house was named Rodney and was the home of retired Admiral Dawson. Previously it was Oaklands, the home of Mr W. Pritchard, Chalford stationmaster. Last century it had been an inn, called The Builders Arms and it is now The Old Builders Arms. The house on the left was the home and shop of Mr Cook, one of the village barbers.

CHALFORD HILL viewed, from the field in front of Rodney House, across upper Marle Hill, in c. 1905. On the skyline to the right is the Methodist Chapel.

Marle Hill,
Chalford.

MARLE HILL ROAD, c. 1910–20, approaching its steepest section dropping to the Bus Terminus at the foot of Cowcombe Hill. Although classified as unsuitable, this road carries a considerable amount of motorized traffic. Some of the cottages are at least 200 years old.

CHALFORD c. 1900. A return to the valley floor with a view west along the A419 from the bottom of Cowcombe Hill. The horse bus has just passed the lay-by used by the County Council to store stone for the road. This was regularly serviced by barge. To the left is the yard of Bliss Mills, filled with stacks of drying timber for the walking stick and wood-turning business carried on there.

HALLIDAY'S OR SMART'S MILL c. 1920s, at the bottom of Cowcombe Hill adjacent to Bell Lock, viewed from the High Street across this narrow section of the valley. This was another mill which had been a woollen, than a silk mill and, in 1912, had become the Meeting Rooms of the Chalford Branch of the Primrose League, used during the war for packing parcels for the troops. In 1920 the mill was taken over by Peter Waals who, on Ernest Gimson's death, moved the craft work of the Gimson School from Daneway House to the mill (pp. 126 & 127) where the work continued until Peter's death in 1937. It is now Arnolds Designs.

CHALFORD STATION as seen across the valley from Rack Hill with Cowcombe Wood in the background c. 1920s. It was built in 1897 on a ledge 60–80 feet above the canal and valley floor. It was closed on 31 October 1964 and, except from a short length of the 'up' platform, demolished by 3 November.

ON LEAVING THE STATION the line curved first right, then left, parallel with the canal as both climbed on their contours up the Valley. This photograph, c. 1910, shows the first curve by the signal box and railcar engine shed. The latter was burnt down on the night of 16 January 1916 and never replaced. The valley twists to such an extent here that the house on the upper left, Westley Farm, seems very much displaced from where one would expect it to be.

THE VIEW FROM COWCOMBE HILL over the station and canal to the New Red Lion Inn and West Rack Hill c. 1900. Centre left is the Bell Inn, demolished some 25 years ago. Many buildings to the right of the Red Lion have also been demolished in the last 50 years.

TWO VIEWS OF THE RACK HILL AREA OF CHALFORD from a de-wooded Cowcombe Wood, showing, on the skylines, parts of Chalford Hill and France Lynch in 1874. The two together show why Chalford has been likened to an Alpine village, but the builders selected good south-facing sites.

EAST UP THE VALLEY, c. 1920s, from one of the Rack Hill footpaths showing Sevilles Mill – demolished c. 1952–3 – and the railway half-viaduct. These narrow footpaths, connecting houses in all the Golden Valley villages, are said to follow old sheep tracks though, today, they are often called 'goat-tracks'.

CHALFORD c. 1900–5. East Rack Hill and Coppice Hill viewed across the half-viaduct and Sevilles Mill. Note how it was necessary to narrow and sharply curve the canal around the Mill Pond because of the limited space available. Upper right is the Baptist Church. Just below is a single-storey extension to a house; Frank Colville's 'Cadover' Photographic Studio (p. 76).

ANOTHER VIEW FROM COWCOMBE HILL over Coppice Hill showing yet another combe running north from the Golden Valley c. 1920. This is Dimmelsdale around the head of which clusters France Lynch.

THE GREATER PART OF FRANCE LYNCH viewed from the Barley Grounds in Dimmelsdale in the 1930s. The church is centre left. The white patch by the trees, bottom right, was the site of a cottage built in 1724 which, in a derelict state, was used by a village gang last century as a depository for stolen garden gates, tools etc. Periodically they would hold an auction sale of their 'findings'! The village elders, in desperation, applied for a police constable to be permanently stationed in the village.

FRANCE LYNCH CHURCH OF ST JOHN THE BAPTIST 1970. The east end from France Grounds. This was framed by a Cedar of Lebanon, left, and a Blue Cedar, right, which had to be felled around 10 years ago to prevent further damage to the east walls of the church.

THE VIEW FROM THE PARISH BANK towards the post office, centre c. 1910–20. Dundry Lodge is on the right. The orchard ground beyond is now the site of the Court View Estate.

AN AERIAL PHOTOGRAPH OF FRANCE LYNCH C. 1962. The head of Dimmelsdale is top right and that of Burcombe (p. 64) top left. Keble road is centre right, while that centre left is Lynch Road leading to the post office in the centre. The field with the dark patch, upper left, is the site of the Chalford Sports & Social Centre. The first house on the right of Lynch Road is Dundry Lodge (see the previous photograph).

SOUTH FRANCE LYNHC viewed from Avenis across the upper levels of Dimmelsdale in the late 1930s. The church is in the trees to the left. The cottages, centre, consisted of a red-brick house/shop, a terrace of four and a pair of semis, all of which were demolished in the 1950s. In spite of warnings of the unstable nature of the ground four bungalows replaced them. By the 1970s one of them had slipped so severely that it had to be demolished.

MOVING THE CAMERA TO THE RIGHT of the previous photograph gives this view, c. 1900, which had barely altered in the 40 years up to the previous photograph. In the last 40 years much of the open ground has been built on. Note the pair of large semi-detached cottages, right.

THE VIEW FROM THE GATE OF THE SEMIS, noted in the previous photograph, towards Butler's Hill and Avenis c. 1920s. The cottage on the right was extensively altered in the late 1930s and renamed Horsepools. The Court House Inn was just off the picture to the left. Note the field on the left with the cows.

CENTRAL FRANCE LYNCH viewed from the field noted in the previous photograph c. 1900. The Kings Head Inn is just off the picture to the right. This view, apart from an overgrowth of trees, is virtually unchanged after 90 years. Note, left of centre, a small collection of corrugated-roofed sheds. These are the ones on the left of the next photograph.

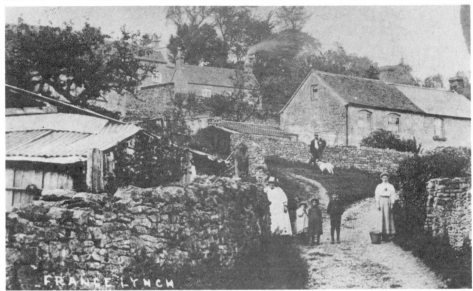

STURMYES ROAD looking north c. 1900. Unfortunately no one has been identified in this picture. The road was named Sturmyes to perpetuate the name of the old sub-manor of Sturmyes Court which occupied the site of the present-day Pontings Farm.

CHALFORD c. 1905. Frank Colville's 'Cadover' Photographic Studio in Coppice Hill (p. 70). Frank was one of the prolific local photographers of the Edwardian Age. During the First World War period he moved to Swindon to open similar studios there.

PROBABLY ONE OF THE MOST PHOTOGRAPHED VIEWS OF THE VALLEY, westwards from Coppice Hill, Chalford c. 1933–5. It shows how narrow the valley becomes as it passes through Chalford and how the railway, canal, river and village street are squeezed together. Behind the three houses on the left the canal bed is dry, already abandoned. A Chalford–Gloucester push-pull autotrain stands in the 'down' platform of the station.

CHALFORD c. 1920–30. The view from the railway at the rear of the old Valley Inn to the entrance to Dimmelsdale. This area is known as Valley Corner and Journeys End. Note that between the two terraces a building is being demolished. This is about where the Boat Inn stood.

CHALFORD c. 1930s. The continuation of the High Street to the east of Coppice Hill, down Tanner's Pitch to the entrance to Dimmelsdale and Ashmeads. This is the start of the true Golden Valley. Note, faint in the background, the skew railway bridge, known as Westley or Jackdaw Bridge (p. 102).

VALLEY LOCK, with the old Water Works building in the trees, viewed from the bridge at Journeys End c. 1905–10. The meadow to the left is now the Valley Playing Field. Coal for the boilers at the Water Works was brought up by barge.

THE NORTH-WEST VIEW FROM COWCOMBE HILL towards Oakridge (faint on the skyline) c. 1900. The light strip lower right is the A419. Centre right is Chalford Water Works and Marley Lane railway bridge. Behind the chimney of the Works is Ashmeads Mill, partly demolished. The Parish and Old Hills woods are on the left.

ASHMEADS MILL viewed from Ashmeads Meadow c. 1890s, possibly late enough for it to have ceased working as a Silk Mill. Only the long single-storey and the two-storey sections remain as a private house. The large house to the left was the Mill House. The cottage in between was the home of Chalford's well-known characters – George & Dorcas Juggins.

ASHMEADS c. 1907. A few hundred yards beyond the mill, opposite the entrance to Bidcombe, stood an old cottage, derelict by this date. It was reputed to be haunted and Frank Colville captured the ghost for posterity! The cottage has been reno-vated and serves as a small barn.

Bidcombe to the Holy Brook via the Hill Villages

In this section we leave the Vale for the villages, built on its northern edge, the chief of which is Oakridge with smaller ones of Bournes Green, Far Oakridge, Waterlane and Tunley.

The combe, called Bidcombe, separates France Lynch from Oakridge and has the small village of Bournes Green at its upper level. It is considered that the area around the village has been a settled area for over 5000 years and may once have been a Stone-Age workshop as numerous part-and fully-worked flints have been found in the locality. The remains of a large Stone-or Bronze-Age earthwork can be seen at The Trench between Waterlane and Tunley. A Roman Villa stood at Lilyhorn at the head of the combe.

Oakridge almost certainly gets its name from lines of oaks growing along the valley edge. Like the other hill villages, the cottages were built on the edges of the old Bisley Common, encroaching thereon in many instances. Stone for them was dug where they were built or else quarried from the Common. This often caused the miscreant to be amerced for 'digging a quarr on the Lord's Land'. The cottages have mostly always been owner-occupied.

For the last 100 years the villages have provided homes and bases for many well–known people who entered whole-heartedly into the village life. Such were the artist Sir William Rothenstein, the sculptor William Simmonds, the poet and dramatist John Drinkwater, Max Beerbohm, the Chancellor of the Exchequer Sir Stafford Cripps and Sir Brian Robertson, Chairman of British Rail. Many cottage craftsmen still live in the villages. The daughter of one of the school headmasters – Margaret Weston – has recently retired from the curatorship of the Science Museum.

AT AROUND 2.30 p.m. on a slightly cloudy Thursday afternoon 25 July 1940, a Ju 88 bomber was attacked by a Hurricane fighter over this area. Machine-gun fire was exchanged, although the two almost certainly collided, perhaps because the Ju 88 was deliberately rammed by the Hurricane. The latter nose-dived vertically through the cloud to crash beside the Oakridge – Bisley Road just clear of the village. At the same time, as the Ju 88 broke cover, a large black object fell from it crashing in front of Pontings Farm House, about 50 yards from the house. It proved to be one of the engines. The plane spiralled to the left to crash on the side of a Bidcombe field. The event, witnessed by SJG, proved a nine-day wonder; the footpaths to the crash site never having been so well-trodden before or since.

THE VIEW FROM THE OAKRIDGE FIELDS over Bidcombe to Old Hills Wood c. 1910. The building upper left is Ridings Farm, the house behind on the skyline being The Cleeves at Avenis. The group of buildings in the trees to the right is the small hamlet of Bidcombes. On the bank of the combe, behind the girl, is the crash site of the German bomber (see the previous photographs).

THIS VIEW, c. 1910, across upper Bidcombe from the Roborough fields at Lilyhorn has not altered greatly in the last 80 years. A few more houses have been built and many more trees grown up. It is still one of the gems of the area.

CONTINUING UP THE GOLDEN VALLEY from the haunted cottage (p. 80) the road forks at Bakers Mill (p. 101) the left-hand road leading up Farm Lane to Oakridge past Frampton Farm. This view south from Oakridge shows Frampton Farm, the haunted cottage on the right and Westley Bridge on the left, c. 1905–15. Ashmeads Mill is behind the tree, the large house, further on being Green Court, near Valley Corner (p. 77).

FRAMPTON FARM, or more correctly, Frampton Place, in 1914. Parts of the buildings are medieval. The building probably originated with the de Frompton family in the thirteenth century. It had connections with the cloth-making industry and Chalford Mill (p. 59) and, under the Twissel family in the eighteenth century, with the mill below, now known as Bakers Mill. Bakers lived at Frampton Place after the Twissels from c. 1740. For the next two centuries it housed farming tenants.

OAKRIDGE c. 1910. Continuing up Farm Lane, at the entrance to the village, this stone trough is reached. It is commonly called the Holy Well, though the well itself is close-by in the garden of Lydays Close, this being an outfall. A well-posed Edwardian scene by an amateur photographer.

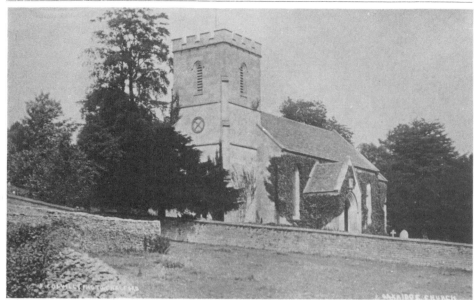

THE CHURCH OF ST BARTHOLOMEW, Oakridge c. 1905. It was the first of the satellite churches to Bisley Church to be built by Thomas Keble the Elder. Building commenced in 1835 and consecration as a Chapel of Ease to Bisley, by the Bishop of Gloucester, took place in 1837. It was given its own parish in 1840.

OAKRIDGE c. 1930. A view east, from the top of Farm Lane, towards the Broadway. On the left is the old post office. On the centre skyline is the Methodist Chapel.

THE OLD POST OFFICE was a single-storey extension shown here c. 1910. It remained the post office until after the Second World War. Mrs Wright, and later her daughter Ivy, were successive postmistresses.

A WINTER SCENE c. 1910–16, from the green at the top of Farm Lane, Oakridge towards Lydays Close, left, and the post office, right. The Dearmer War Memorial water trough was to be built soon afterwards where the fence is on the right.

OAKRIDGE c. 1905. Mary Gardiner's Cottage in Chapel Lane – the lane running from below the Butchers Arms to the Methodist Chapel.

OAKRIDGE c. 1920s. A view from Sammels Hill towards Cobden and Hillcroft (the centre buildings). The latter was John Peacey's (p. 162/3) Bakery. As elsewhere in these Golden Valley villages, these narrow roads and footpaths have been given names of villagers who once lived near them.

OAKRIDGE C. 1900. Mary Twissels' Cottage in Twissels Hill. Presumably it is Mary sitting at the door. She lived there with her brother Benjamin and died a spinster, aged 76, in 1904. Benjamin died the following year, aged 68, as a result of a fall from a haystack. The cottage was sold and, in 1910, renovated by H. Gardiner, the Oakridge builder. It was, possibly at that time, called Golygfa Hardd (beautiful scene). In 1940 it was sold to Mr N. St Clair White and renamed St Clair.

OAKRIDGE C. 1900. Jane Young's old house, in a delapidated state, whether through neglect or fire and neglect, is not known. The path connects the Broadway with the upper road. A bungalow was built on the site around 25 years ago.

OAKRIDGE. A panoramic view of the Broadway from above the Whiteway. The date can only be estimated but is believed to be early this century.

OAKRIDGE c. 1910–20. A view from the field below Whiteway Cottage to the Old Mill House. It is a right-hand extension of the previous photograph. On the skyline, centre, is the 'pine' end of the Butchers Arms.

WHITEWAY COTTAGE, now Whitespring, at the junction of the Broadway and the Whiteway c. 1910–20. Some readers may recall Micky (Wiggy) Spencer who lived there 50 years ago.

OAKRIDGE c. 1910. The view from the bottom of 'Beccas Hill over the Broadway to the Golden Valley at Westley Bridge. The group of buildings to the left of the haystack is Frampton Place. Penn House, at the top of Farm Lane, is to the right. The Old Silk Mill stood in the area behind the right-hand wall.

OAKRIDGE C. 1910. The path which connects the Broadway, near the Old Mill, to Chapel Lane. It is known as 'Back of Ollis'. The Old Mill House is behind.

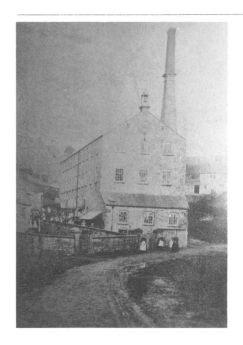

'BECCAS HILL runs up to the right of the building to the Chapel (faintly top left) c. 1880. The Mill was built by the Clothier, Nathaniel Jones, of Chalford around 1840/5 to provide local employment. It is said that he did so to alleviate the problem of the girl employees having to walk to his mills in Chalford in all weathers. It was a silk mill for most of its working life, closing in 1890, sold in 1897 and demolished soon afterwards. Being steam-powered, coal was brought by barge to Bakers Mill Wharf and brought up Farm Lane by horse and donkey.

THE WESLEYAN CHAPEL, Oakridge c. 1920. A Mr Pickersgill, a local preacher of the Stroud Circuit, has been called the founder of the chapel. His name is associated with eight others in an indenture of 1791 which might indicate the completion date of the first building. Various cottage meetings had been licenced as early as 1742 but a Revd William Jenkins of Gloucester seems to have been the first Wesleyan Minister to preach at an open-air meeting on the edge of the Common before 1790. The land on which the chapel stands was sold by a William Jenkins to William Webb and eight others in 1797 so, perhaps, he was that minister and had originally bought the land for the chapel. This building replaced the first in 1874.

HALFWAY BETWEEN OAKRIDGE AND WATERLANE lies the Pest House shown here in 1895. Originally built in 1779 by the Bisley Feoffees as an isolation house for inmates of Bisley Workhouse suffering from smallpox, this use seems to have lapsed with the building of the Stroud Workhouse in 1837. In 1895 there was a severe outbreak of smallpox in Stroud, brought by a tramp, and it was resolved to open the Pest House again. Feeling in Bisley ran so high that the 'ambulance' conveying the first case was attacked and turned back. Before police arrived the house was set on fire. Four rioters were sentenced to between one month and one year hard labour. The house has been a farmhouse for most of this century.

WATERLANE CROSSROADS C. 1900–5. The lady in the Victorian dress is Mrs Seth Gardiner. The road behind her is the old road from Stroud to Cirencester (p. 54). The house behind the tree was the Crown Inn, adjacent to the lane leading to Watercombe.

WATERCOMBE HOUSE c. 1900–5. It occupies the site of two or three dwellings which were listed in wills of the eighteenth century as Watercombs. It lies above the valley of the Holy Brook.

THE WEST END OF FAR OAKRIDGE from the Oakridge road c. 1910–20. The Nelson Inn, now Birds Frith Farm, was on the left of this photograph. The view is over the valley of the Holy Brook to Sapperton whose church can just be discerned to the right of the maypole.

FAR OAKRIDGE C. 1910. The cottages on the lower road to the village green. These were converted by the artist Sir William Rothenstein into a large house which he called Far Oakridge. He used local masons, tilers and carpenters for the conversion. For many years he and his wife took an active part in Oakridge Community life, especially in the Village Players.

THE VIEW OVER THE FRITH COTTAGES, now The Frith, across the valley of the Holy Brook towards Edgeworth C. 1910–20. The cottage to the right in the distance is Sherra at Tunley.

TUNLEY c. 1900–10. Frith Farm on the Waterlane Road, just before the Holy Brook is crossed. It was modernized and enlarged by Sir Stafford Cripps after the Second World War and was his home for many years. A common sight was to see him jogging round these lanes in the early morning.

TUNLEY c. 1890. The same cottages as in the next photograph. In the left-hand doorway are Mrs Gardiner and her second daughter Mary. In the right-hand doorway is Mrs Bucknell. The two girls are Mrs Bucknell's daughters Sophie and Annie. Mrs Gardiner and Mrs Bucknell were sisters.

TUNLEY C. 1900. The view on entering Tunley from Waterlane and Far Oakridge after crossing the Holy Brook. The old road from Stroud to Cirencester bears left here up Tunley Lane; that to the right continues to Daneway. The house is now called The Old Forge, being converted some 40–50 years ago by Dr Snow from a pair of semi-detached cottages. The right one was the home of Mr William Bucknell, the blacksmith.

TUNLEY C. 1900–10. A part of Tunley hidden from the Daneway road and approached from Tunley Lane. The little Methodist Chapel, which served Tunley in those days, is at the rear.

HILLHOUSE LANE, leading from Tunley to Daneway, in the summer, c. 1900–10.

Bakers Mill to Edgeworth

This section is, perhaps, the most unspoilt length of the Golden Valley, having Frampton Mansell and Sapperton on its southern rim and Edgeworth on its western flank after it swings towards the north at Sapperton.

For about one and a half miles from Bakers Mill only the River Frome, here little more than a small brook, and the canal occupy the valley floor. From Sapperton only the little river holds sway in a comparative haven of peace even in these modern days.

All three villages are old, Sapperton being a Domesday village. Sapperton and Daneway will probably always be remembered as the villages to which Ernest Gimson and Ernest and Sidney Barnsley came in the 1890s to practice their ideas of craftsmanship. The craft skills they encouraged in many of the local youths are perpetuated in their descendants today. They all lie buried near the entrance gate in Sapperton churchyard. Sir Robert Atkyns, the seventeenth-century Gloucestershire historian, also lived and died near Sapperton and lies buried in the church.

BAKERS MILL C. 1910–20. The view west across the canal reservoir to the mill and house. This was not a millpond but a true reservoir, built by the canal proprietors to store water collected from the River Frome and the springs around Oakridge. Below the white fence on the left is Bakers Mill Lock, the footpath above leading to Westley Bridge.

THE VIEW WEST FROM PUCKS MILL LOWER LOCK to Westley Bridge across the Manor Grounds which are squeezed between the railway and the canal c. 1920. The Manor House lies behind the viaduct. The house in the distance is Little Hattons with Hattons behind the tree. A branch of the Bliss Clothing family lived at Hattons in the eighteenth century and W. Baker of Frampton Place (p. 84) rebuilt part of the house in 1844. During renovations in 1936 wallpaper was stripped off one wall revealing faded writing which showed that the house had belonged to the Hancox family for 436 years and formed part of the Daneway Estate (p. 127).

WESTLEY BRIDGE 28 August 1963. The 'up' mid-day express approaches the bridge. The photograph shows why it is sometimes called Skew Bridge. Note the GWR Automatic Train Control Ramp in the 'down' line. The site above the bridge to the right was once a secret meeting place for seventeenth-century Dissenters.

FRAMPTON MANSELL *c.* 1920. The north-east view from behind the Manor House towards the signal box and level crossing (upper centre). The break in the skyline level of the woods is where the valley of the Holy Brook runs north.

FRAMPTON MANSELL *c.* 1920. The view from the west end of the church north-west over the house which is the present day post office. The viaduct, right, well-known to railway buffs, was an original Brunel-designed wooden structure. It is believed to be the first in the Golden Valley to be encased in brick *c.* 1859. Seen faintly over the viaduct is the valley road leading from Ashmeads to Bakers Mill (p. 84).

FRAMPTON MANSELL c. 1920. The north-west view over Frampton Farm, as it was, to Avenis (pp. 75&84). This is not to be confused with Frampton Place, which is the white building, upper centre. Faint over the farm buildings is Bakers Mill, the depression in the hills behind being Bidcombe.

THE VIEW NORTH ACROSS THE VALLEY to the Taut at Oakridge c. 1920. The footpath, running down the depression past the white shed, connects The Taut with Pucks Mill in the valley. This path was called 'Bread Hill' and is said to have been made by unemployed men who were paid, for their labours, in bread made by the Oakridge Baker.

THE NORTH-EAST VIEW FROM THE WHITE HORSE ROAD towards the Crown Inn – the building in the distance, extreme right, c. 1920.

FRAMPTON MANSELL c. 1910. The Church of St Luke, built in 1844 to the design of J. Parish. It was threatened with closure several years ago, but was saved by a few dedicated villagers and neighbours. It is now one of the churches in the oversight of the Rector of Sapperton.

FRAMPTON MANSELL C. 1930. The view down Pike Lane towards Bidcombes and Bournes Green in the far distance. The building on the right is the Baptist Church (p. 155).

FRAMPTON MANSELL C. 1930, the opposing view up Pike Lane. The village hall is just beyond the bend.

THE VIEW EAST ALONG THE SAPPERTON ROAD towards the Crown Inn in the 1920s. The building on the right was, at this time, probably the post office. Unfortunately nothing is known of the family in the photograph.

FRAMPTON MANSELL c. 1905–10. A closer view of the Crown Inn taken by the Chalford photographer, Frank Colville. The shape of the Crown from this angle has altered little in the intervening years, the bulk of the alterations having taken place at the rear. The village stores was later to be sited in a building erected in the garden of the cottage to the right.

THE 'UP' MID-DAY EXPRESS approaches the western portal of Sapperton Tunnel, 28 August 1963. This photograph illustrates quite well the width of GWR tunnels necessary to take the old broad gauge.

FRAMPTON MANSELL c. 1910. The track leading from the Crown Inn, over the railway level crossing, to Pucks Mill. The way the valley twists above Chalford is very apparent in this photograph. The buildings, centre right, are at the bottom of 'Bread Hill' (p. 104).

PUCKS MILL, viewed from 'Bread Hill' c. 1890s. This old mill was a woollen mill as evidenced by the round teasel-drying house. It is doubtful if it was ever a silk mill, but it is believed that machinery was taken from this mill to equip Oakridge Mill (p. 93). It was bought by the Canal Proprietors to safeguard the supply of water to Bakers Mill Reservoir. It was demolished around the beginning of this century. The house on the right was the Oak Inn. The house to the left of the mill was the millhouse.

PUCKS MILL AREA, again viewed from 'Bread Hill', with the Oak Inn central just beyond the canal bridge c. 1910. The building, extreme left, appears to be an altered round house.

THE OAK INN at Pucks Mill viewed from the canal tow-path c. 1910. Mr & Mrs Elliott would have been the licensees. After closure as an inn in 1923, the building lapsed into use as a barn etc. for Puck Mill Farm (Mr Peart) but has now been restored as a dwelling.

AROUND TEN YEARS AFTER THE ABANDONMENT OF THE CANAL, this photograph of Whitehall Lower Lock, in the late 1930s, shows the dereliction that rapidly ensued. The lengthmans cottage was still lived in. After abandonment it became derelict but has now been restored.

A NORTH-WEST VIEW FROM FRAMPTON COMMON over the canal as it curves between Whitehall Lower Lock and Whitehall Bridge, bottom left, c. 1910. After crossing the bridge the rough track from Daneway enters the valley of the Holy Brook and then meanders up the hillside past Trillies to Iles Green and Far Oakridge on the skyline to the right. Trillies is an ancient farm once in the possession of Cirencester Abbey.

WHITEHALL BRIDGE, a north-east view from the River Frome meadows c. 1930. The path above the bridge ascends the hill through Siccaridge Woods towards Hillhouse Lane (p. 100). These woods are now a nature reserve, the site of wild lilies of the valley, among other plants, and are known locally as the Lily Woods.

A SOMEWHAT MORE IDEALISTIC VIEW of Whitehall Bridge looking down the canal, but with barely enough water to float even a canoe c. 1910–15.

The Locks, near Sapperton.

THE VIEW WEST FROM DANEWAY WHARF LOCK, the upper lock of the flight of six which dropped the canal from Daneway Basin to Whitehall Bridge c. 1910–15.

ANOTHER VIEW WEST from the Wharf Lock, or Upper Siccaridge, Lock c. 1880s. Something of a puzzle photograph because it has the appearance of a Colville photograph which would date it some 20 years later.

THE VARIATION IN THE DATE (c. 1890 or 1905) is because such a photograph could have been taken before or after the restorations of 1897–1903. The view is east from the Wharf Lock through Daneway Bridge to the Summit Lock. Wharf Cottage is on the right and the Bricklayers Arms is on the left. Note the horse waggon by the inn; it appears to be laden with sacks of grain or flour.

DANEWAY SAWMILLS with the millhouse beyond c. 1900–5. The mill was then owned by the Gardiner family. It was in this mill that Ernest Gimson, on his return from learning the craft of chair-making from Philip Clissett at Bosbury in Herefordshire, received permission to set up his pole-lathe and work it by water-power. He was given the use of young Edward Gardiner to turn the parts for him. So Edward learnt the craft of chair-making, which he carried on in later life at his own workshops near Leamington. The mill closed around 1914/15. The steam engine of the works was moved by horse waggon – nine horses and in two loads – to the mill at Shipton Moyne, near Tetbury. It is believed it was sold again later to some Works in the Chippenham – Warminster area.

A SIMILAR VIEW over the Wharf Cottage to the Millhouse and Daneway Hill c. 1910. The hill road was cut as a road to improve access to the canal and tunnel workings during construction of the latter.

A WINTER VIEW from Daneway Millhouse across the Wharf and Basin and down the valley to Frampton Mansell c. 1905–1910. The track to the left parallels the canal to Whitehall Bridge on its way to Far Oakridge.

THE CANAL BRIDGE and Bricklayers Arms (now the Daneway Inn) viewed from the bottom of Daneway Hill c. 1905–10. Plenty of raw material, for the sawmill, on the right.

DANEWAY, The Summit Lock in 1917. Sapperton Church is on the skyline. Note how the canal curves to the right following this contour of the valley to enter the tunnel underneath Sapperton village. The valley then begins to curve left towards the north to its head near Brimpsfield.

A VIEW ACROSS THE GREEN to the cottage where the architect Norman Jewson lived, c. 1905–6. Early in this century he came to Sapperton to work with Ernest Barnsley, completing Ernest's major work of the building of Rodmarton Manor after the deaths of both Ernest and his brother, Sidney.

THE VIEW ALONG THE VILLAGE MAIN ROAD towards the church corner c. 1905. The village school on the left was where the well-known book, *Village Heritage*, was compiled by the headteacher and scholars.

AN OPPOSING VIEW from the church corner with the school at the bend of the road c. 1905. Immediately in front of the school the entrance to the village lower road can be seen. Are the children the same as in the previous photograph?

THE LOWER ROAD to Sapperton church c. 1905. The first building on the right of the road was the village stores. Again are the same children in this photograph? Very possibly as they were all taken by the Cirencester photographer – Dennis Moss.

THE VILLAGE SHOP C. 1905. The advertisement on the corner of the shop is one for Frank Coville, photographer. What was the BIOTUS advertised by the window?

SAPPERTON 1934. The spire of the Church of St Kenelm undergoing repair. The present church stands on a very old church site and was largely rebuilt in the fourteenth century from its earlier Norman shape. Other alterations followed in the fifteenth and sixteenth centuries, while the nave and transept were rebuilt by the Atkyns family in the early eighteenth century. The chimney of the heating chamber, which is on the north side, looks somewhat incongruous, being brought from Henwood Mill (p. 128) when it was demolished.

AN INTERIOR VIEW OF THE CHURCH — the south transept, aisle and gallery c. 1927/8. The bench ends, with carved Jacobean figures, were taken from Sapperton Manor House when the first Earl Bathurst had it demolished in c. 1725–30. The monument in the south transept is to Sir Robert Atkyns, the Gloucestershire historian.

Post Office, Sapperton.

SELF-EXPLANATORY, but it seems that, even in Edwardian times, there was 'time to stand and stare' c. 1910. A lovely mellowed old Cotswold cottage serving a useful purpose, opposite the Bell Inn.

SAPPERTON VILLAGE HALL 1912. It stands opposite the Bell Inn. It was built to the design of Ernest Barnsley, assisted by Norman Jewson, and shows their dedication to the Cotswold style. The hall is said to have been built in 1912, but the original postcard was dated 22 January 1912 suggesting that the opening was close to that date and that this photograph may have been taken before the interior was finished.

SAPPERTON C. 1900. The Bell Inn, which is still the only village pub and a well-known and very popular watering hole. The board shows that Stanley Harrison was landlord at this time.

A VIEW FROM THE GARDEN OF THE BELL across the valley to Oakridge c. 1930. The angle of the view is somewhat deceptive for, in the upper left quadrant, the white building is the present-day Daneway Inn.

SAPPERTON c. 1933. The Leasowes – the cottage which Ernest Gimson built for himself, c. 1902–3, with its original thatched roof. This photograph was taken about 14 years after his death when his wife, Emily, still lived there. The thatched roof was destroyed by fire in 1940 and is now tiled.

SAPPERTON c. 1905–10. Beechanger – the house which Sidney Barnsley built for himself c. 1902–3. When the friends moved from Pinbury Park (p. 131), Earl Bathurst allowed them to select a plot of land in Sapperton on which each could build a house for himself to his own design.

SAPPERTON c. 1910–15. Upper Dorval House – the house which Ernest Barnsley built for himself c. 1902–3. The site chosen was more sloping than those chosen by his brother Sidney and Ernest Gimson and also had an old cottage standing on it. So he altered the old cottage by the addition of a large wing either side.

SAPPERTON C. 1902–5. The view from the field below the church down the valley, showing how the valley begins to turn towards the north. The cottage is the lengthmans cottage at the mouth of the canal tunnel.

DANEWAY 1916. The view from the sawmills over the Summit Lock to Daneway House.

THE ENTRANCE TO DANEWAY HOUSE 1917. Some of the outbuildings used by Gimson are on the right.

DANEWAY HOUSE in the 1930s. The Manor House of the ancient Denway, or Tunley, Estate – the two names were interchangeable. The oldest part of the house pre-dates 1339 when the inhabitants, Henry de Clyfford and Matilda his wife, were granted the right to have an oratory there. The Hancox family occupied the house, as tenants and owners from 1397 to 1860. The five-storey addition was an extension of the early seventeenth century. William Hancox, of that time, was said to be a Captain under Cromwell, being with him when he expelled the Rump Parliament in 1633. Another descendant was Thomas Hancox who was present at the opening of the Thames & Severn Canal by King George III in 1789. Part of the canal, of course, ran through his estate. He was said to be a big and powerful man and once easily lifted an offensive individual over Daneway Bridge and dropped him in the Lock. On his death his daughter inherited the property and, on her death, the estate passed out of the family. It was sold to William Dangerfield (p. 30), who sold it to William Chapman, Silk Throwster of Chalford, who sold it to Charles Smith of Chalford, owner of the Victoria Steam Joinery Works (now Chalford Chairs) who sold it to Earl Bathurst around 1897. He commissioned Ernest Barnsley to restore the house and, in 1902, let it and the buildings to Ernest Gimson and Ernest Barnsley, who moved their furniture craft workshop from Pinbury Park (p. 131). The outbuildings became the workshops and the house was used to display their furniture. Soon after Gimson's death in 1919 the house passed into private ownership.

HENWOOD MILL C. 1900–5. This old mill, now no more, appears to be in a very isolated spot in the valley, the River Frome on the right being little more than a stream. Yet, until the new road from Stroud to Cirencester was cut across Minchinhampton Common in 1746, this was the point where the old road via Bisley, Waterlane and Tunley crossed the Frome, going up the hill to Park Corner and Cirencester.

EDGEWORTH – the Church of St Mary c. 1910. The building contains traces of its Saxon forerunner, the nave and chancel being Norman. It was extensively rebuilt/restored in 1860–70 with the usual Victorian fervour. Like many old estate churches it stands very close to the Manor House.

THE INTERIOR OF THE CHURCH c. 1910.

EDGEWORTH MANOR HOUSE C. 1910. In the early seventeenth century the estate belonged to Sir Henry Poole, a Royalist, of Sapperton. In 1650, the Parliamentarian Nathaniel Ridler, who was lessee of the Chalford Estate of Corpus Christi College, bought the estate. His son, Nathaniel, rebuilt the old house at Edgeworth completing the work in 1685. Two centuries later the house was again altered and enlarged to give it the form shown in these two photographs.

PINBURY PARK 1933. Situated on the east side of the Golden Valley opposite Edgeworth, again on an ancient site. The medieval portion is believed to lie hidden in the main part between the gable ends. The historian Sir Robert Atkyns lived here until his death in 1711. It became a farmhouse and, by 1890, had fallen into disrepair. In 1893 Ernest Barnsley leased it from Earl Bathurst and repaired and altered the house and gardens before moving in with his family. His brother, Sidney and friend, Ernest Gimson, renovated an adjoining farm building into two cottages for themselves, and the outbuildings into workshops. In 1902 they moved to Sapperton and Daneway and Earl Bathurst took over Pinbury Park as his residence. This photograph was taken a week before John Masefield, the Poet Laureate, took up residence there.

The Nuns' Walk, Pinbury Park.

PINBURY PARK C. 1910. Why the 'Nuns Walk'? The manor of Pinbury had belonged to the Abbess of Caen and, later, the Abbess of Syon, who retained possession until the Reformation. There is a legend that the ghost of a nun haunts this avenue, rolling a Double-Gloucester cheese along it!

SECTION SIX

Golden Valley Life

No display of old photographs would be complete without a selection of village life, illustrating individuals, groups, sports teams, school classes, shops and work-places, organizations etc. So here is a selection of photographs from the life of the villages along the Golden Valley. More are included for some villages than for others, only because village size varies and also because we have more pictures of certain villages. We believe the names we have given to individuals in these photographs are correct and we thank all those who have so kindly helped in their identification.

THRUPP SCHOOL AFC 1937/38. Left to right. Back row: C.H. Poole, B.G. Bishop, W.J. Kelsey, K.G. Loveday, J.C. Tanner, K.C. Chandler, N.E. Hampton. Front row: J.E. Jeffries (Headmaster); J.O. Savage, M.V. Tanner, A.K. Hozier, R.E. Kerry, D.N. Bond, F.J. Riddiford (Master).

BRIMSCOMBE SCHOOL GROUP 3, 1927. Left to right. Back row: Joan Phillips, Grace Heaven, Joyce Blanch, Evelyn Marsh, Joyce Castledine, Stanley Townsend. Middle row: Osmond Stephens, Gerald Beard, Jim Prime, Marjorie Farmer, Ernie Farmer, Bill Dickenson, Basil Evans, Bill Heaven. Front row: Rene Dean, Joyce Phillips, Peggy Banks, Edna Blanch, Doris Tranter, Vera Dean, Betty Baglin, Cyril Tilley.

BRIMSCOMBE STRING ORCHESTRA, 1920s. This was formed and tutored by Mr Travis Cole, who described himself as 'Instructor of Orchestral Training Classes by the Polychordia Method for the Bath & Bristol Co-op Society, Glos. Education Committee, etc., etc.' He lived in Victoria Road, Brimscombe, and formed many other such orchestras around the Stroud area, e.g. at Amberley, Edge and Nailsworth. In this photograph, Mr Cole is on the extreme left and Mrs Cole is on the extreme right in the back row. The violinist, seated left front, appears to be Mr Marmont, Headmaster of France Lynch Church School (p. 149).

Bottom, left.
BRIMSCOMBE SCHOOL c. 1931. Left to right. Back row: Leslie Davis, Bill Dickenson, Ron Bateman, Phyllis Close, Bill Heaven, Dennis Brown, Arthur Beard. Third row: Bill Ponting, Leslie Neal, Peggy Banks, Mary Kennedy, Vera Dean, Bertha Young, Doris Tranter. Second row: Eric Darby, Jim Bond, Joyce Castledine, Ivy Close, Alice Close, Marie Brown, Barbara Feldwick, Evelyn Marsh, Miss Poulton. Front row: Pam Lodge, Edna Blanch, Olive Close, Ken Dyer, Joyce Phillips.

GROUP OF OFFICIALS AND FRIENDS at the re-opening of Brimscombe Polytechnic by Her Grace the Duchess of Beaufort on 5 October 1911. Left to right: PC McKnight, A.W. Hook, U. Hook, Lawrence Grist, Tom Weaver, Miss Massey, Mrs F. Aikin-Sneath, J.H. Smart, W.C. Randall (Headmaster), H.S. Evans, E.H. Evans (Founder), E.C. Chivers, F.C. Aikin-Sneath, PC Neale, F.E. Critchley (County Councillor).

BUSSAGE c. 1905. Harry Wall was landlord of the Ram Inn (p. 35). He also ran a business hiring out horse wagonettes etc. Every year he organized a treat for the village children, transporting them somewhere local for a 'bun-fight'. His son, Jack, on the left, always wore coachman's dress on these hired wagonettes, complete with post-horn. Harry is the driver.

Bottom, left.

BROWNSHILL c. 1901. The Sisters of Bussage House of Mercy with guests. The Community was founded around 1850 by the Revd Suckling, Vicar of Bussage, Mrs Grace Poole and Bishop Armstrong, as a penitentiary for girls to get them away from the environs of Stroud Workhouse. Mrs Poole, called the Mother Foundress, carried on the work until she retired in 1898. She died in 1900. After a short break to decide the future of the Community, the house became a branch house of the Community of St Mary the Virgin, Wantage. One condition of this 'takeover' was that new launderies and drying rooms should be built. This was agreed and the new extensions were opened in October 1901 when it is believed this photograph was taken.

BUSSAGE WOMEN'S INSTITUTE, posed outside the village hall, 1930s. Mrs Fownes-Luttrell, on the extreme right, was the aunt of the present owner of Dunster Castle, near Minehead, Somerset.

BUSSAGE VILLAGE SHOP at the top of Bussage Hill oppposite the Village Green in the late 1930s. Mrs Davis and her daughter.

BUSSAGE AND EASTCOMBE CO-OP STORES, a branch of the Stroud Co-op Society in the 1920s. Mr John Clissold, Manager, and Joe Doughty. It is now a private house on The Ridge.

THE OPENING OF THE WOMEN'S INSTITUTE HALL, Bisley, 1922/3. It appears that some potential members and 'associate' members are seated at the front.

BISLEY BLUE COAT SCHOOL in the 1950s.

BISLEY 1930. The floral wreaths for the Dressing of the Wells ceremony on Ascension Day, held by the children and helpers in the school playground before the start of the procession through the streets.

BISLEY 1907. A different parade this time – the Church Parade, descending George Street *en route* for the wells. Almost certainly it was Bisley Brass Band leading.

BISLEY 1938. The South Cotswold Beagles move off from the Bear Inn along the Stroud Road, under the watchful eye of the Master Geoffrey Sanders.

CHALFORD c. 1920s. Bennett's Wheelwrights premises on the upper floor of Clayfields Mill adjacent to the A419 (p. 58). George Bennett is on the right with his sons Bert and Bill. George's father had been a wheelwright in Butt Street, Minchinhampton.

CHALFORD c. 1905–10. Taysum's Blacksmithy on the A419 opposite Chalford Church (p. 60). Left to right: William Taysum, Alf Maisey, Harold Taysum (William's son), -?-. Two unknown lookers-on have wandered into this photograph.

CHALFORD C. 1925–30. The interior of Peter Waals Workshop at Halliday's Mill (p. 67). The photograph is taken from the road doorway. Three almost completed pieces of furniture can be seen. Those people on the left of the photograph have not been identified but those on the right, beginning from the front, are: Ernest Smith, Harry Davoll, -?-, Owen Scrubey, Percy Tanner, -?-, Percy Burchett, Peter Waals.

Bottom, right.
CHALFORD HILL C. 1910. The workshop and yard of E. Hook & Sons, one of Chalford's builders, at Randalls Green. When the business closed, some 20 years ago, the building was demolished and the site developed as the small estate of Anthony Court. The shop, extreme left, became the Butcher's Shop of Harry Peacey and is now that of Paul Dutton. Fred Creed Snr is in the cart, Hector Hook is holding the hand cart and his father, the owner, Gus Hook, is on the right at the top of the steps.

CHALFORD C. 1910. William Gardiner in the doorway of his General Stores in the High Street. The shop next door was run by his daughter, Ellen, as a Drapery etc. The entrance to Sevilles Mill was just round the bend of the road, the tall building on the right being the only part of the old mill buildings still standing.

CHALFORD HILL c. 1910. The present-day Chalford Hill Stores with the then owner, Frederick Steel, in the doorway. A shop front which has altered very little in the last 80 years.

CHALFORD HILL c. 1915–20. Just above Fred Steel's Shop was the Bakery of Matthew Workman, who was succeeded in the business by Mr Stares. Here, Mrs Stares is standing at the gate of their small shop, well-known for years by schoolchildren as a sweet shop. Around 20–25 years ago the shop was extended and modernized and the railings removed to create a hard-standing. The shop closed, as Pincott's Stores, in 1988 and is now a private house. A Cotswold stone wall is at present being built along the line of the railings.

CHALFORD HILL c. 1930. The Commerical Road Stores of Harold Gardiner, son of William (p. 145). As can be seen, something of everything besides just groceries and provisions. The Stores closed some 40 years ago and is now a private house – Clematis Cottage.

GLOUCESTERSHIRE SPECIAL CONSTABULARY, Chalford sub-section, 1943. Left to right. Back row: E. Peacey, J. Taylor, H. Hook, W. Dalby. Front row: E. Griffin, L. Freeman, Spec. Sgt. C. Lambert, PC J. Bailey, H.R. Mallinson.

CHALFORD CHRIST CHURCH SCHOOL, Group II, 1924. Left to right. Back row: George Sturgess, Leonard Abel, Cyril Hemming, Jim Turner, George Peachey, Austin Taysum, Harcourt Dowdeswell, George Small. Third row: Flossie Davis, Vera Beard, Rene Fry, Phyllis Kirby, Nellie Bedwell. Second row: Leslie Earl, Jessie Mills, Evelyn Baker, Winnie Fry, Majorie Stagg, Mildred Grimmett, Rosina Ricks, Sylvia Padin, Phyllis Mills, Omar Cottle. Front row: Ronald Etheridge, Sidney Goodyear, Tom Jones, Stanley Cottrell, George Bowns, Fred Williams.

CHALFORD HILL SCHOOL, c. 1922. Left to right. Back row: Mr F. Webster (Headmaster), Wilf West, Rene Holmes, -?-, -?-, Reg Clarke, Len Freeman, -?-, -?-, G. Staddon, J. Dutton, -?-, -?-, Ivy Stares, Miss Ethel Phelps. Third Row: W. Holmes, L. Bidmead, Winston Browning, F. Hayward, Don Pritchard, Lionel Gardiner, Len Jewell, K. Hale, Vera White. Second row: R. Stratford, M. Phelps, B. Williams, R. Gardiner, E. Stafford, G. Allen, Len Peacey, -?-, E. Minchin, Dennis Wright, Arthur Coventry, Winnie Bidmead. Front row: -?-, Kathy Barnes, Evelyn Jones, E. Armstrong, -?-, Evelyn Pegler, -?-, Kath Gubbins, P. Garrett, Enid Rowles.

CHALFORD BRASS BAND, c. 1908. Left to right. Back row: E. Davis, Sam Gardiner, ? Greville, Tom Davis, ? W. Young, Walter Wood, -?-, Seated: Alex Cook, -?-, ? Hayward, Walter Gardiner, Archie Hawkes.

FRANCE LYNCH PHILOMUSICA SOCIETY. 1920s. Left to right. Back: Blanche Young, Reg Young, Dennis Workman, Len Blizzard, Ron Blizzard, Mr Marmont, John Steel. Front: Joan Butler, Keith Jackson, Dolly Davis, Sidney Sharpe, Olive Creswell, Florence Workman, Ron Blizzard, Freda Minchin.

OAKRIDGE c. 1910. The Maypole Dancers in the Vicarage field. Sixth from the right in the front row is Mary Gardiner (now Mrs Aldridge).

OAKRIDGE SCHOOL, First Class, 1923. Left to right. Back row: Joe Tanner, Ted Bucknell, Bill Long, Norman Bucknell. Third row: Kathleen Gardiner, Gwen Hunt, Rose Gardiner, Daisy White, Winnie Davoll, Mr Snowdon. Second row: Lily Fern, Majorie Gardiner, Mona Wood, Muriel Hunt, Doreen Seabourne, Rosemary Smith. Front row: Robert Fern, Victor Hunt, Linda Gardiner, Ethel Bridgeman, Shaun Robinson, Arthur Phipps.

OAKRIDGE SCHOOL, 1933/4. Left to right. Back row: Dennis Stump, Leslie Stayte, Leslie Hunt, Winnie Fry, Violet Hunt, Joyce Hunt, Hilda Gardiner, Miss Tombs. Middle row: Jack Fry, Alec Woolls, Harry Hunt, Stewart Young, Bob Tuck, Percy Osborne, Kathleen Stayte. Front row: Ethel Hawkins, Mavis Young, Madeline Blackwell, Grace Dean, Eileen Powell, ? Bown?

Bottom, right.
OAKRIDGE C. 1905–15. A village custom. It was common practice for villagers to keep a pig or two in a sty in the garden to be fed on household scraps, and 'meal' if it could be afforded. It would be killed in the autumn, usually by one villager renowned for his pig-sticking skills, the hair burnt off on a straw bonfire and, finally, it would be carried into the shed on a makeshift bier to be dismembered and salt-cured for the family table for the winter. Here, the deed having been done, John Peacey (left) and John Bateman (right – pig-sticker) carry the carcase in. This annual event gives rise to the following:

> Dearly beloved brethren, is it not a sin
> To peel a potato and throw away the skin ?
> For the skin feeds the pig, and the pig feeds us,
> Dearly beloved brethren, is it not thus ?

OAKRIDGE C. 1945. Helpers at a Methodist Chapel function outside the schoolroom. Left to right. In the doorway: Mrs Dawson. Back row: Mrs N. Bucknell, Mrs Daisy Gardiner, -?-, Florrie Bateman. Middle row: Florrie Wilcox, Mrs Dangerfield, Mrs Farmer, Miss Powell. Front row: Violet Wear, -?-, -?-, -?-, Nancy Bucknell.

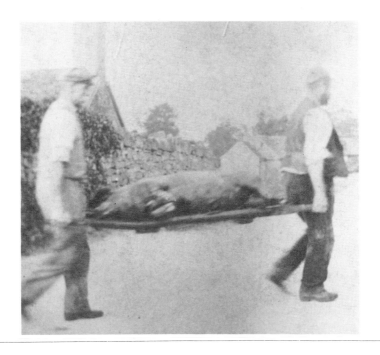

OAKRIDGE ORCHESTRAL SOCIETY c. 1910–20. Left to right. Back row: L. Griffin, W.E. Blizzard, D. Minchin, Sid Young, F. Webb, Hollis Gardiner, A. Ingram, A.G. Gardiner. Front row: W. Wood, M. Webb, P. Stratford, Sid Gardiner, Scott Young.

FRAMPTON MANSELL 1887 or 1897. Queen Victoria Jubilee celebrations in the old barn near St Luke's Church.

FRAMPTON MANSELL 1924. The erection of the Baptist Chapel in Pike Lane. In the wall of the chapel a Memorial Stone, for those of the village killed in the First World War, was laid by Brigadier General Fasken, of Hyde Grange, Chalford, on 23 February 1924.

FRAMPTON MANSELL 1930s. Mr Arthur Roberts.

FRAMPTON MANSELL c. 1910–20. Percy Watts in a donkey cart outside the Crown Inn. It is thought that the man leaning on the wall beyond the donkey's head is Mr Ben Baxter.

SAPPERTON c. 1915–20. Schoolchildren posed not far from the Bell Inn. Left to right. Back: Majorie Baxter, Annie Lewis, Grace Harrison, Ida Harrison. Front: Sid Harrison, Maggie Lewis, Bobby Baxter, Dorothy Lewis.

MRS ELIZA HARRISON of The Bell Inn, Sapperton, c. 1900 or earlier.

SAPPERTON MORRIS DANCERS performing at Cirencester (?) c. 1920s. Left to right: Frank Whiting, Jack Harman, Alf Cobb, Reg Whiting, Frankie Gardiner (hidden), E. Cobb.

OUTSIDE GIMSON'S COTTAGE at Pinbury Park c. 1895. Left to right: Sidney Barnsley, Miss Lucy Morley, Ernest Gimson, Mrs Ernest Barnsley, Ernest Barnsley with his two children.

MRS EMILY GIMSON c. 1920s.

MR SIDNEY BARNSLEY in 1926. A photograph taken by Edward Barnsley at Froxfield on 5 April 1926, i.e., three months after his brother Ernest's death and five months before his own death.

A GROUP OF CRAFTSMEN AND APPRENTICES employed by Ernest Gimson at Daneway House Workshops c. 1905–15. Left to right. Back row: -?-, Peter Waals, Percy Burchett, Harry Davoll. Seated: -?-, Fred Orton, -?-, -?-. On the ground: the boy would have been a starter on sweeping up, name not known.

ACKNOWLEDGEMENTS

For the majority of the general views, as always, we are indebted to the local professional photographers: Colville, Comley, Elliott, Lee, Major, Merrett, Moss and Stone, as well as the national ones: Taunt and Frith and those who followed in their footsteps. But had it not been for the amateurs, happily clicking away to record family and village scenes, this record would have been very much the poorer. Yet none of what you have seen could have been put in this book had not so very many people – friends, colleagues, acquaintances and those unknown to us until they contacted us with the offer of yet more material – so willingly allowed us to copy their postcards, snaps, family albums, etc. Nor must we forget all those who have drawn on their memories, and those of their families, identified so many in school groups, etc. and recounted tales of village life of many years ago. Several such as Fred Hammond, Ray Kimber, Geoffrey Sanders, Ray Smart and Duncan Young have passed on, taking with them a wealth of local knowledge. Not so well known, perhaps, to readers is the co-operative spirit which abounds among local historians and family researchers, which often results in odd snippets of information which enable one to complete a caption. In this respect we are indebted to Juliet Shipman, Jocelyn Blanshard and David Viner to name but three.

In the photograph credits which follow we hope that we have not omitted anyone who has loaned the originals of our copies shown in this book and we thank them for allowing us to use these copies.

Misses A. Adams ● Barnsley ● D. Brimfield ● Leach ● A. Liddiatt ● S. Padin
S. Tanner ● J. Tuck ● Wallis ● Mesdames Bishop ● J. Blanshard
Clements ● Cook ● Cottrell ● Y. Crew ● Dangerfield ● E. Dugdale ● A. Fowler
A.M. Gardiner ● F. Hale ● Hemming ● Hendy ● I. Jackson ● I. King
M. Maidstone ● H. Marsh ● Martin ● Niblett ● M. Norris ● Shepston
J. Shipman ● Smart ● F. Smith ● A. Strange ● J. Sturm ● Thurston ● Tod
Townsend ● R. Whiting ● Y. Williams ● J. Young ● Dr R. Allen
Messrs G. Allen ● H. Beard ● L. Blizzard ● L. Brown ● B. Carrington
D. Clarke ● H. Clarke ● R. Clarke ● P. Clissold ● A. Cobb ● R. Cratchley
F. Creed ● E. Cuss ● G. Damsell ● T. Dangerfield ● W. Dickenson
M. Fenton ● P. Gardiner ● J. Garner ● G. Gleed ● M. Goodenough ● E. Harper
L. Harrison ● H. Hook ● H. Hunt ● R. Kimber ● F. Lloyd ● W. Merrett
M. Mills ● F. Peacey ● H. Peacey ● D. Pritchard ● J. Riddiford ● H. Roberts
M. Rose ● G. Sanders ● J. Smith ● C. Stagg ● J. Stephens ● I. Thomas
R. Turner ● K. Wear ● R. Whiting ● G. Young ● W.D. Young.